THE
SAND
GARDEN

by

THOM NAIRN

This one for Jock
For all you've done
for all of us
Cheers
Thom
August 14

THE SAND GARDEN

This edition published in 1993
by Dionysia Press
20a Montgomery St
Edinburgh EH7 5JS

Set by Dionysia Press

Cover design by Thom Nairn

Cover printing by Let Us Print,181 Bruntsfield Place,
Edinburgh

Printed in Scotland by Dionysia Press

ACKNOWLEDGEMENTS

Acknowledgements are due to the editors of the following publications where some of these poems, or mildly deviant relatives, originally appeared: *Cencrastus, Faultlines, Fox, Envoi New Writing Scotland, Northlight, Other Poetry, Prospice, Spectrum, Understanding.*

Other poems included in this collection were also recorded for broadcast on Scottish Television's In Verse series.

THIS
ONE
FOR
CARMEN
HELEN
AND
PATRICIA

CONTENTS

PART ONE: FROM WANDERING

PART TWO: STRATEGIES.   22

PART ONE: FROM WANDERING

OREOCEREUS NEOCEISIANUS

The white-whiskered cacti,
  Old craggy men
On dilapidated porches

Thigh deep in dry gravel,
They say nothing
And have no pipes.

Here,
    Smiles are possibilities
    On which we can only speculate.

Their worlds are carefully the same,
    No alien stimuli, the unexpected
    Is not permitted.

Their patience is inestimable,
    A viewable spectacle,
    Ambiguous example.

Slowly sequestered
In the streets' callous galleries,

In this meticulous aridity,
    Who among us
    Will pass out first?

LINING UP THE WORLD

Blood red
Chasing dark dreams through slick cells,
Watching gristle from our thin skins
From living passages,

Cyclic, vibrant, violent
As a coiled and calculating cat
Far from asleep
On blue nights in black like these,

When buildings slyly gauge.
Each other's dimensions,
Bridges defy rivers, rivers bridges,
The world's pieces eye each other up,

Sometimes you can see the threads
And know, as in whispers,
The moon defines its own suspension.

TRAVELLING SIDEWAYS

Opening my eyes suddenly from a shop doorway,
500 cc's of bike, of metal and plastic
Is travelling sideways, in black sparks it's screaming

Hard and bad at the road: this is noise in imitation,
Cold mechanics on stone, emulations of burned
And flayed flesh.

And the two riders, also travelling sideways,
Clumsy dice, careering, long soft and tumbling,
Skidding, burning their expensive leathers, swapping
Dead flesh for their own.

These things do not happen in slow motion,
But they get to a halt, begin again, one runs
To the other, stunned, technically undamaged.

Fast travelling cars just behind have seemed to opt out,
Phased out and fast cut, travelling as billiard balls
On expensive video, pause- freeze-frame- colon:

Hundreds of eyes from the Christmas crush home-in,
And these two rough, tumbled and frayed aliens
unite the whole, very long, broad and crowded street,
Well, for maybe most of a moment.

SEEING MAYBE IN A DOOR

Hard and warm inside
But the wind and rain
Move regardless,
Making a chaos outside
Like people
Not wanting to drown
And maybe seeing a door.

NEURONS

Up among the hills, the steel stark spire
Of the radio mast
Crackles and sparks in the frost,

Far below in the valley, the cottages,
Up from the earth as if rooted there,
Close shuttered for the night, these
Places where people huddle fire-watching,
The fast flicker of flame and shadow
Catching faces, white in black.

And under heavy-lidded skies
Impartial
As
Oceans
Our world's
Interminable twitching.

5

CARNIVAL JAZZ
(For Carmen)

Winter; dawn comes late, easing out of the night,
Light comes as slowly as my eyes open,
Stretches its grey look over the quiet land.

As slowly as my slow legs, my stiff arms, reach
Out over long sheets to meet your warm hand,
Meeting me, telling me, your eyes are open
And more.

But you can give and I can take much more,
As I can give and you can take much more,
Than the light from the land, the land from the light.

The land stirs slovenly
And humphs and shrugs
A mountain range
As grumpily
As a crumpled quilt
And muffles eyes and ears,
Embracing silence and shadow
Far harder than light.

Old lovers gone tired and slow: but here in your arms,
Even with me gum-eyed, blind, hung-over and ugly
Your hands signal volcanoe, tempest, vortex,
You're carnival jazz with black eyes that never sleep,
Over-looking two small landscapes: yours, mine.

You make me
A land of two moons
With no hunger for silence,
I can only rise for you,
Embrace the light
As the light
Should take the land.
You feed me more,
Make me grow in
Ways I now know
And thought I knew.

LONGSHOREMAN

Celan,
Walking without sound,
Always on lonely shores,
Casting out bottles

In which
Are encased
The short lines
Of the dead.

SLICES

While I walk
The dark slopes
Of the ploughed earth
At twilight -
The furrows
Are sharp and harsh,
Rough and grubbing
At my brown boots -
The old brown dog
Lurching - panting -
Scanning out on my right -
Chest and face rising
In his billowing breath -
(The sky is swollen
With snow -
The warm grey
Of a pigeon's belly -)
Below by the loch,
Snug as a worm,
The old broch
In its rough
Hewn cycles
Nestles like a child
In a shelve
Of the hill,
Alone -
I look over
My shoulder -
As I move on
I cut a rough wedge
In the hard frosty air,
Rough and sure
As a cleft in peat,
As dawn walking
In heavy ryme.

ROPE-WALKERS

In a grey sky
Over old snow
These gulls are acrobats.

They perform their wide-limbed harmonies,
Rope-walkers,
Over a hill's piebald back,

Now that the sun
Has
Opened for heat,

An eye from
A hand
Of fingers unclenching.

VAMPIRES
(For Patricia)

The bat swings incurious, a black and rum-eyed
Pirate, scurvy and skeletal in the
Vein-spanned rigging of two wild wings:

Hillsides are always different places
At twilight

On silence:

In a corner you're out cold as a child,
Fingers around your mouth, body
Reaching into a shell,
But your eyes are made up into black,
Your full lips are lush and red.

Shoulders like known interlopers
Reach up over you, to possess and to hide.

The sound of the sea comes from the shell
In all our opening ears, coming out in flowers,
Sucking up fast and safe as semen.

The grumbly fricatives
And scarring colours,
The bat's wings around
Our blackening eyes
And surfacing bones.

The rumbling of all our years and fears,
A crumbling for powders,
       for colours,
To bigger and sharper pictures,
Inviting to try, to make new things
From old if damaged fixtures.

LOW NOSE TRASH STYLE

The night and the moon clap hands
And the frost snaps up corn like a hungry rat.

Moon rolls a low nose on lower hills
And splits a smile cheap gangster trash style,

And no wide cut brimmed hat
To shallow the eyes
But he's satisfied
Flips a match and passes by.

And the sky opens creaky long-legged
Dripping down its juice
All smeared tall-fingered in the trees
And the trees green-lipped do not smile

But eye up the sky in a long, low sneer
And leer, wary and scared
New lovers, cheap gangster trash style,
Gone old and cold in the dawn.

ACUTE

Her tongue like a moth
Flickered in my mouth,
We tasted our warmth
A taste of its own.

She left
Soon after that
For we both knew

That her husband
Too
Has a keen sense of smell.

SHOW-TIME

Children move like heavy wagons

Down the silence of the theatre.

Three thousand people pretend

Another three don't exist,

And their failure is wonderful.

THE TAKE OFF
(For Alasdair Gray)

Old buttressed fortress,
The decal edge
Zip-toothed on a blunt saw,
These catch the crackle
Of sunny crenellations

As eyes flash on motion
From a train

Or the light through
Closely spaced railings
Catches a ripple as you pass.

This is illusory motion,
But who would try if
They couldn't believe
The world moves behind them?

This is just poems
And unlikely tales,

You need the pattern to be
Just on the eye's corner,
Just so you know

It is there
And can't be caught,
Sometimes like flies are supposed to,
These things take off backwards.

EDWARDIAN GRASS

The Chinese orchestra,
Dedicated energetically,
Rehearse their cellos,
    Their violas
    At 4.00 a.m.

At 4.00 a.m.
Their fragmented slashes
Scar and furrow,
Furtive as foxes,
Sharp sound-shadows
Massed and shimmering
Across a vast expanse
Of this warm, moonlit,
Edwardian grass.

THESE STOMPERS
(For Jarv)

Bent as hooks or moustached,
Black coats
As twisted cones,
These men are burnable.

Against this, hawks have nothing,
Bones themselves
Have extensions
Known only to frogs.

Urban evolutionary masterpiece,
These stompers,
Legs pulse and beat
To match the heart.

On pale grey bar-room skin
The dark and dusty robes
Cowl depths of coldness within,
The eyes
Are black, pragmatic probes.

BENDING THINGS

A woman
In the village
Of Zoogocho,
Has been gathering maize
For four thousand years,

Her skin is copper
and the maize is yellow,

Together
They celebrate the sun.

REMEMBER ANTWERP 1568

I'm always around,
You know me fine,
I watched Bruegel paint his lepers,
Their thick lips and dumpy stumps,
In party hats and foxtails
With filthy linen covering cuts.
I was there : carnival, Antwerp 1568,
Under a lousy archway gate
With a rumble in my guts.

I'm always around,
You know me fine,

I crawled the bars with Ben Jonson
When they wouldn't put him on
And he'd sell his boots for a pittance
In the cause of a jar and a song,
And sure we sold his potions,
London 1625,
Trying to stay alive.

I'm always around,
You know me fine,

That old tight bastard Charlie
In the fog and the shit and the damp
Taking
Notes up blind alleys,
In top coats, whiskers, tails and a gamp,
I watched from the gutter
In the shadow of a lamp,
I was there too - London 1852.

I'm always around,
You know me fine,

I've been thieving with Villon,
I've fucked Jean Genet,
I've been drunk with Dylan Thomas
And MacDiarmid on Whalsay,
I've tramped sometimes with Rimbaud

When we made it Paris or bust
And I've trekked Soho with Quentin
And the rumble in our guts.

I'm always around,
You know me fine,

Hong Kong and Sydney,
Bombay to Marseilles,
I'm the bastard scavenger
That stands in your way.
I'm every parasite
Around the kibbutz,
And if you sleep, I'll wake you
With the rumble in my guts.

I'm always around,
You know me fine,

Piccadilly Circus,
The Bowery or Brest
Fine you know me
You bastards,
I'm one of the best;
Edinburgh- Grassmarket
On a seat with some wine,
Aye, fine you know me
You bastards,
I get you every time.

RUNNING HOME
(For Angie)

Edinburgh night in the rain,
The streets in the wind and neon
Are black-polished glass.

Street lights and
The bright eyes of cars
Are caught as stars
In black waters.

We're three, huddled in a cab,
Cold travellers on a strange sea,
The winds batter around our doors,
Unfriendly hands
Reaching for our spines.

We hold to each others' warmth
But send out our eyes
To take in the night
With us: running home.

The sharp black and neon
Still a flicker in our eyes
As later
We make a feast of the fire.

FROM WANDERING

In our uneasy silence staring,
Too tired
In our eyes to try,

We're too unsure of
Where we stand
To risk talk
And clarify why,

Who's with who tonight?
Is she with me
Or with her?

On the inner city bus
In the late night,
We sit in
The cripple seats,

Legs dangling,
Our faces in black glass
Are surreptitiously
Examining,
Who's she watching?

My thighs flattening
On the green plastic,
Self-consciously
I brace the muscle.

I want her to want me
And I know
We're all as scared
Of the stopping
Half a mile on
Through the rain.

PART TWO: STRATEGIES

STRATEGIES

1

The Dawn's square pale grey
Rising in the boxed window.
A tangible rising,
A dark, wet image
Sliding into being
In the photographer's shallow tray.

The city's low traffic growl
Opens slowly on solos,
A bike or a truck
Passing singly in the half-dark,
But growing steadily,
Sound on sound into deeper sound,
The long low grumble
Of the city's daily ensemble.

Days as years and lives,
Turn, grow and fade
In the same cyclic ways,
From a birth, from a winter darkness
Into gradual light.
A summer's growling apex,
Then on and back
To the night's square pale grey
Rising in the boxed window,
Watched by an old man
Anticipating the still cold
And silence of the winter's night.

2

The snow much softer than sand
Sifting slowly in low wind
Makes white beaches
Of the long, dry gardens,
Desert shores of light
Come creeping in the night.

Vast and quiet as cats,
More silent than skies:
And no steps intrude
To offend eyes drifting
Silent from dull windows.

Drifting ships
Over smooth seas
And no horizons,
Just the white glare
Cancelling
The day's sad ambience.

3

To a moon of tattered wool
Or a cataract eye,
The kind of eye
A battered face
Could grow around:

And with the cloud
The growings come,
And with the wind
The strange jaws move
Their soundless changings.

Light now furrows brows
Or flaring cheeks,
Puckers jawlines,

Then darker motions
Take the light,
And the wind's manoeuverings
Obscure its own
Discursive achievements.

Here now below,
Curled and wired as a cat,
The city unfurls
New strategies
To create and defeat.

PICKING UP SIGNALS

The dust and dead tambourines
Under the empty stage,
Sweat smells of
Old and battered bean bags,
Wrinkled tennis balls
Punched into cups
And faceless voices
In an empty hall.

Constellations on a
High hill as pivot,
The frost
Bringing out stars
To take everywhere,
This is all subterranean,
Dragons are in the cracks
With the spiders,
Co-exist with children moving
Their arms like scales.

Mute they breathe,
Minds move
Their own pictures,
Here there is only
Motion -
Gabbled semaphore,
Arms toe to fingertip,
Moving arms like scales
With no gauge.

EQUALLY-BEAKED

Out there
The dawn has turned around.
Careful renegade
Turning a trail.
Without a sound
Trees vanish in the dark.

And in here
Now figureless,
The stripped clock's
Spindles armless
Spin time pointless,
Stripped bare and boneless

Birds now treeless
Turn in time,
Black with clockless figures,
Birds and fours equally beaked,
Roundness matching heads,
Folding wings in sixes.

Jumbled and dense as bees or water,
Sand in the wind,
Dust in the sun,
They spell for us
In fast immaculate silence,
Knowing we cannot read.

TWO FLAT MILES OF SILENCE

The river is still
Unmoving
Cold as steel-

Mist filters the sun
Restrained
Slight and above life-

Light
Gives polish
To the steel

Sweet sheet cold
And gleaming
Over two flat miles

Of silence-
The familiar black
Stacks beyond in flames

Mist
Catches the fire
Mirrors the smoke-

The bridge here
A long limbed
And tangled bird

Angles itself
Sharp and raw
On the river's ice-white.

CONFRONTING

Four foot nine in a five foot coat,
She waves fast and points like a politician,
A mangled and bushy bonnet
Crammed on her wrinkled, bobbing head.

Lean, tough, growling, but not as hard as animals,
This is violence signalling frailty,
This is the bite and barks don't need mentioned.

She points and he points and it's known
From various angles, there's no point.

He's high walled and buffered

In a battered burger-wagon: Princes Street 14/3/89,
Aproned arms waving in diverse directions,
He'll not have her exist this much,
I'd like to think she knows about him, but:

Her mouth moves fast even with her back to me,
From the top of a traffic-bound bus
And from long flat ways all around

We watch, I watch: mime artists enacting lies
And consequences, tricks and tatters.

Watching continents through keyholes does nobody any good.

SO DREAM
(For Carmen)

A little red wine
And watching the moon
From Spain.

Quietly on the side of the night with you,
Your arms could be my own warm wings
Around both our shoulders.

That close, we could just glide and glide
And move
Away,
Move away.

A little white wine
And watching Spain
From the moon.

PSYCHOCANDY

Needle-nose and the head an eye lidless,
Skin-shaved in black and chains: the skin is grey.

Beat-up boots, far from careful rags,
But still, arms clenching like a baby,
Tight around shackled shoulders,
Whining here through tears

Around broken glass, heaped dead diamonds,
Scraped and pissed on walls,
Dead booze in stars of dark stains
On dry concrete:

Jesus and Mary Chain: Barrowlands,
The one cop on the door,
Not too fat but clean and safe,
Working hard with his eyes
On different directions.

Smug and calm doormen in
Fresh shirts and smirks,
They'll not have this in here,
Too gone for these guys.

For all the blades and tatters, tattoos,
Booze blues smack and shit,
This cop's unreal:
He is not here, works at it,

And your sweat shirts and smirks,
Bastards: enjoy your wives and homes.

"Tell them son, no me".
"Ah telled thum, Ah telt thum."
His fists are hearts convulsing,
On and on and on.

GAMBLING
(For Charles)

His black eyes and elbows

Poised on air,

Groin churning, he peers

Up the skirts of the

Block-metal machine,

Trying to anticipate

And calculate the run

Of the heavy fruit inside.

It bam-bam-bams away

And smiles

With cherry teeth for him,

He presses the buttons,

Manipulating, rubbing

Lower limbs to its cold thighs,

They gleam at each other

In mutual understanding.

ANIMAL HEADS

The apples lay in the desert,
Brown cows' eyes in animal heads
While
(unobserved)
A road began
From the sand,
Buildings quietly assembled
Themselves from warm rock:

Leaves came,
Hot harvest rats
Heading for holes:

As long arms
Unravel
From the sands,
Each accompanied
By long nailed hands,
Two passing camels
Stop in the sun,

Consider each other's
Astonished eyes,
Blink and bow
Their blunt brown brows
And jackass jaws:
      Munching apples
With yellow teeth,
They continue.

CAMELS

A cool, warm dawn
And camels rise like cranes
With sharp teeth
And hidden tracks
To bite and shamble,
To give the dawn,
      the sand
      and drivers
A day they deserve.

And tourists gather snapping
As flies around some
Lurid, immobile meat,
Unaware of how it is
To deal with camels
Dealing with sand
And drivers
And dawn and dust
And teeth
That never stop
And the chaos
Movement can be.

PRIVATE AXIS

The old bar leans out its long arm,
Nearby, tall machines wink sly acknowledgement,
Close conspirators in their silent cynicism.

The old
And battered man
Arches, circles, reels,
Coils in on himself,
Dervish drunk and
Tracking out his private,
Invisible axis.

On the threadbare,
Darkly patterned carpet
He reads his fading,
Fragmentary mandala,
His magic is dying
And it is not alone.

On the periphery of the bar's long arm,
Overlooked by tall and cold glass shelves,
Bottles on bottles fill the stadium,
This man looks like coming to harm.
A slow fan turns its dark eye,
Incapable of telling a lie.

    The people watch
    And
    Touch their mouths
    With glasses,
    Framing eyes in absence.

The circles grow relentlessly,
His passage, inscrutably centrifugal
On this terminal cycle to silence.

NO ONE BOTHERS TO IMAGINE

In the low mists climbing over the city,
The city has no tongue
Now
And speaks only lightly
In scrambled hieroglyphics
Like this wasted stone,
Rashly assembled and abandoned,
Severed signals to forgotten recipients,
The empty towers mime significances
No one bothers to imagine.

In the half-night, the city,
The city has no tongue
Now
The stones here look on
As cold and long-eared skulls
Of other islands,
And only the same cold songs
And histories unsung, unspoken.

In the dawn, the day,
Rabbits and children, passing strangers,
Track out their superfluous paths,
Gouging their hazy maps of passage
With no sense;
And over that
The
City growls its messages,
Growls out here to the stones and towers,
Scenarios, scores in stores and hordes
For us to taste in the night,
In the low mists climbing above the city.

DEBATABLE INVISIBILITY

In the slow movement of another still room,
My own lives, in slow kaleidoscope, whorl too
Fast and bleak for any eye's correlation
    (let alone more)
Sound may be a constant, the cumulative
Impression is dangerous transience.
There is no peace in sound when you listen
    (that hard)
The implications jar and grate with the things
Too often present, places you need spaces for,
The sounds, like punctuation, only emphasise
    (things that won't exist)
I am here of course, however invisible
You or I may wish me to be: like it or not
This is a construction, we have each other
    (but only you can stop)
Or is it just me? Are you still there ?
    (I won't care if you won't)
Poetries can be mixtures of mystery, misery, celebration,
Right now I just want to say I refuse to believe so little exists
    (like this).

FAMILIAR STILLNESS

A table's non-Celtic whorls
Chasing non-existent moons
Into
Non-existent galaxies.
Light is only half-way here,
The rain and the city
Unintentionally
Providing their own unique backdrop.

Your nails and tall fingers
Prickle my spine at midnight,
In its own stillness
The night speaks for me.

My own places
Are just so,
Just as transient,
Midnight
Losing or gaining in
Its own ineluctable transience.

Your presence like a cat
Denies itself,

Here in this familiar stillness,
Spanish eyes and stranger dreams
Intrude, belie our lying.

Your breathings are bellows
That echo my chest.

Spaces between stars may be like this,
A knowing of being somewhere
And not,
Altering the shapes of our eyes.

MOST OF ALL THIS

The leaves are dead fish in the wet black stone,
   (Between these are the shadows of stars)
Walking over these things the earth is glass,
   (The stone's a battery, sucks up the night)
Thin glass, piranhas and drowning only
   (It backs up on you, hard water, cool life-wash)
Millimetres away, odd way to walk,
   (Eyes and ankles attached by threads, just)
Scary how your own life's decisions can
   (Cut in around like bagatelles can to)
Ripple your spine before you're too
   (Aware of the sky, horizon or too)
Sure you're in your right world, let alone mind

Or awake: and there's only your eyes on
Your feet and the thin skin, trees breathing
Down your neck, cars growling at themselves in
The remnants of other people's silence. So
Into the thick morning of buses and
Warm smoke upstairs, top-deck, three faces like
Familiar dumb moons looking from their
Own wild cold places, or reaching for mine.

Most of all this is somewhere else, where
The nectarine sucks in its puckered cheeks,
Blows out dusty golden light soundlessly.

TALKING TO ANYONE
(For Bill)

She'll talk to anyone
Non-stop
As she wheels and deals.

Junk scrap and rags
In black poly-bags
Add up to twice daily meals.

Whatever she feels - it's no matter,
Saturdays she drinks
And tries not to think.

Sundays she sleeps
And thinks,
One day this'll be for keeps.

Mondays to Fridays
She trails the streets
Checking on deals,

Practicing patter,
All in all
It could be worse.

Just the same,
Whatever she'd rather,
She remembers the rules.

Keeps her best manners
For the horse, just like
Her father before her.

WOOLLY-CLOTHES

You wear your silence like a trenchcoat,
Obvious, a kid in a ballaclava,
So, everyone knows
When your coat passes,
Knows the colour,
Anticipates the itch of your ballaclava.

Your eyes are made up as your silence,
Triple-bluff, a flaunt
That mostly you can lose,
Too much you want the hood
As well as the mask
To pass for your face
And still deliberate
The wrong response.

It's like the hawk with its hood,
But you don't know your target:
Motion,
Warm meat,
Is not enough,
You want to keep the mask
And eat.

ISLAND NIGHT
(For Marion)

Here the night

Is heavy as glass.

Glass and its space,

Two litre capacity.

It's that empty

Kind of night,

You are wildly asleep

As I walk

In uncertain silence,

An island night with no wind,

I move and walk, bead of

Sweat over folds of fat,

With the slow touch of

Perhaps advancing hearts

Reaching and deepening

The uncertainties of solitude.

FLAT-SAND

That one
Dry sandy
Palm.
And the sky spreading
Out as if spilt and blue.
The palm hide
Ruffled cool still
Peristalsis as the
Trunk of an elephant.
The leaves' long silk
As green as tears
To touch
The rough hide
Like a rhino's
With soft
Pale fingers,
You can feel the pores
Dry hard and sharp,
With the pool
Sandy troughed
Among scrub.
Until,
Five miles away
Across flat sand
And sky,
The old tin and
Cardboard bus
Leaves its dust-trail
Like a stain.

THE ONLY LIFE

A dying bonfire,
Orange side of red,
Still with sharp edges
Of flame. Snake tongues
     And
     Red lizards
     In rock.

Only life now
On a low stubble field,

Caught in a corner
Of the eye's darkness,
Half asleep at the wheel,

I look down from a truck
High above on the M-way.

PART THREE: THE SAND GARDEN

WITHOUT WORDS

A warm silence.
The failure of
Minds and words.

When words fail
and even eyes, our hands,
Can't do what's needed.

How do we
Speak and move
And touch, even into ourselves.

Tracing tired echoes
Of the moon,
Never smiled in its life,

Been with me, cut through me
A long time.
Is everything and me, that far away?

I like to think
I'm warmer and closer than that,
Mostly I have my doubts.

Endings are a strange place
To hinge beginnings
When the past is so opaque.

The future is as cool,
Round and unpredictable
As the moon and its touch.

After midnight:
Scrapings at the bottom
Of a small barrel.

SHOUTING AT HARBOURS

The stone rain on a still pool.
Bird's sound on claws in the sand.
Dead fish heads, coral, slate, cold voices.

Gulls and clothes whiplashing
Quiet cars away
With the cold slush of waves.

The small and white dead crabs
Are irregular smears
On the wet leather-black rock.

Nearby,
Men are shouting at the harbour,
Dark, slick and not listening,
Stone faced.

Worlds won't move or
Adopt accommodating forms
For men's voices.

But still, their boats bang as bones
Against the quay endlessly.

INTO THE SUN

Through a scummy Edinburgh window.
it's the edge of half-light
with a red sun sending out arms.

And the crags on the edge of vision,
looming from nowhere,
suspended, stalled
in a murky pane of glass.

Through a dark-red but misty vision,
Mars
looms like a monument:
we're cut loose.

Voyeurs in a wheeling and sealed pod,
veering around worlds
we only have colours for.

Transportations triggered in the
flicker of an eye,
when ceilings and walls dissolve
and something in you
moves somewhere else.

The floors fall away into the sun,
every tendril you have

reaches to the roots of trees,
maps flow in your mind like stars,
star-patterns catching anatomies:

then you break a surface
into another now
and space folds away
as the illusions
of your Self as a child,
the different you;
Mars is back in the sky,
night's come.
You're in a room and it's time for blinds.

FINDING DISTANCE
(For Patricia)

Kissing you
As I leave
Before dawn,
I don't know
What
Your eyes see,
Your lips feel.

I can feel
Your skin,
Your shape and form,
Your body's bed-warmth
Inches away: kissing you
As I leave
Before dawn.

Sometimes
I know,
You are more
My woman
Half asleep then,
Before too vividly,
The world rolls in.

You shake off
Your innocence and warmth
With the blankets,
Sometimes
Fight me
As hard
As the dawn.

THE MARK

Fresh in a sharp steel cast
And hard as a wire this neck,
And like the swan,
This dry, patterned limb,
The moulding of a pummelled head
Designed and coiled in beaten lead.

The tongue is silver-
Only the sun moves
On eyes cut
In cold, slick glass.

In a quiet hunger,
In the shadow and stone,

Waiting for the mark
And flash of warm meat
To conjure animation.

OBLIGATION

Things come down
To shaving bones,
Peeling down bone
To slick cool moons
On pale carpets
In smoky rooms.

But these are just echoes
Of remembering,
Even simple things,
Of the really bad dreams,
Of runnels of sweat,
A half scream in the night.

However strange
And wild the scene
Your mind is designed
To try at least
To wipe itself clean,
However far
Minds may move
From sleep.

DRY HARBOUR

We'd come over the crest in the last of a low sun,
Breathless, rough and grubbing through the heather,
Scree and the scuff of sharp rock on lean leather.

Beyond the tumbled and scrawled heap of the cairn
The world slips down and away over the Tay
With only shadows and half-formed glimpses
Of the city's towers and shifting sprawl:
Amorphous with inexplicable movement, only a stain
In the light on the land like water.

As the day fades night mists move from trenches
Like commandos, camouflaged they creep around curves,
Move in staggered clusters, long grey figures
Searching, wary and prowling around us.

We move down to the barren cottage
Thinking about not believing in ghosts or
The remnants of souls shackled to cold stone,
Knowing this is one place we're wasting our time.

That people lived here, effectively nowhere,
Roadless and sunk deep among low hills,
Cannot be questioned at this hour,
Whatever's left beyond this gutted shell
Communicates itself quietly, insistent.
The usual senses are irrelevant
And here we both know it as
We too, reach each other differently.

The low winds here chill and whisper,
Move fraught with anticipated voices.
Warily we walk over and around
The remnants of low walls.
Stuttered brick and flecked stone rubble
And the mists move with us, around and through,
Making notions of our own shapes dubious too.
Through tall grass and long dark weeds,
Battered cans, the remains of tables, of shelves.

And uneasily we both see in each other's eyes
There's more here than domestic debris,
Dead history
And the shallow scars of tramp fires,
Moving us away tonight, only just,
Gently and firmly.

BALD-HEAD

With his woolly neck
And trenchcoat,
Old bald-head
Ahead of me
Three seats,

Hair and wild wax
In his ears, a mess,

Shoulders slumped
and stained
As old mattresses.

Through the front
Bus window
The front hooves
Of Wellington's
Rearing horse

Glance back
Wet light
In the sun,

Small at this range,
They correspond
Precisely,

Dimensions mark
For mark
With his woolly neck,

His bald-head,
Tricky image
For early morning,

Same way painters
Dwarf and figure
Cathedrals
With a thumb.

AFTER THE FIRE

The fire-swept hills
Take miles
In the reach of the moon.

We sit on the periphery.
As if in the gallery,
This perspective

Cannot be entered,
Black and tiny bats
Sweep around our faces,

We are animal eyes
Surrounded by flies,
We do not need told
This world is theirs.

THE NIGHT AS IT COMES
(For Betsy Dunn)

The old wood-shed
Dark and rotting
Timbers more piled than built
Black in the rain
And soaking up the night as it comes
Down dark with the rain

All around the trees
Brush noisily at the sky
Wave their cold arms
Casting off leaves like gloves
In the wind.

The old ash path winds off
Indifferent among
The gooseberry bushes,
And at its head
She stands,
The torn apron
Blown wild in the wind,
Looking up knowingly
At the sky.

FREEZE-FRAMED

You've lost your dark power,
    I've lost mine,
In each other's eyes
    We're too translucent,
These are things we know
But can't quite spell.

Once we were both masters,
    Equally opaque,
Now, and we do know,
    We walk on rails
    We don't see
    But both,
    Deep back,
Acknowledge.

We've conceded each other's mystery,
Maybe cancelled is closer to history.

Too little left to see
From the
Too much we do see
Where we stifle,
Muffle,
Conclusions.

And here we are,
Both
Playing stupid games
Of tig and tag,
But we're both
Stone statues of ourselves
And mallets are such ugly things.

TALL TALES

Trees here unseen by axes,
Fossils lie ungathered,
Leaves and dark tracks
On the earth,
Dry skulls and bones
Grow shiny in the shadows
Around black and wordless eyes.

It is winter
And only crows
Talk and clatter,

Lions and ghosts co-exist,
Tell each others' stories
Until the blue dawn comes
Making its light and sound.

Moss moves its small stems
In green arcs
Sucking at the sky,
Time unfurls here,
Its depths unclear.

SHE LOOKS AHEAD
(For Lesley)

Wide and brown as a plum
She carries her child,
A packet or parcel
Skin-tight and round,
Tiny, smiling, toothless
Without sound.

Her eyes are black-rimmed,
Deep and dark,
She looks ahead and walks slowly,

Beginning already to know,
Intricate, accurate,
Spinal spiral severe as a leaf
Gnarled in first frosts.

Wide and brown as a plum
She carries her child.
High-eyed and deep-skulled,
Feeding in that darkness
Uncaring,

Carrying with her
Her life
As if a precious toy,

They are strange
And tenacious,
Will not let go.

WHEN THE LONG TRAIN'S GONE

The night-tube time,
   When the long train's gone,
   Doors snapped tight and taken
   The air, the sound, the people.

So you're left stunned alone
   In too much space,
   A part of the brickwork,
   A stone bollard,
   A torn poster
   Coming to rest
   From the rush,

   No longer valid,
   The show long gone.

TUNNELS

As night mines your dreams
For darker signs,
Too sharp shadows
Of endless echoes,

Even the simplest worlds
Can get too big for you,
Too high and loud and narrow,

Night tunnels your sleep
With darker dreams,

Cold corridors,
Hospital pallour,
A faceless mirror,
An empty grate,
Endless corridors
To stranger places still.

Yet still the treasures come,
Centre-floor around cold corners,

A jam-jar with
A butterfly,
Living unstifled
At the
Dungeons' cold core.

LIFE UNDERWATER

To a slight light
From the smooth summit

The city is swathed in mist
No shapes are spared

Focus moves
As the mist moves

We are in the gallery
And these motions are endless

Down there is a mind's life
Underwater

Light makes its own casts
As surely

In that light
We all have our touch

Only a slight light
Can define

If the mists move
There's nothing to see

In these swathings
We take our lives.

MARS

Leaning deep, heavily catching shallow breath,
Sharp, old and stale, pale red,

The dry skin flushed, coughing dust and debris,
Asthmatic in the dubious air:

The five senses dulled,
He holds to untouchable walls
Like a drunk.

Watching sun and stars
Through hazy eyes, sensing echoes
Of the night's black, cool breeze
Coursing through the heavy grooves
And furrows of his brow.

Alone and empty these days,
Age comes ugly in awareness of decay.

NOBODY'S HOME
(For Dr Donald Allan)

Nobody's home but me,
in a way anyway.
The Sun's been busy,
notching out the hills
to canvas clarity,
too still,
this kind of light could kill.

Edging around the shades
it comes, it cuts you out,
I can see my dimensions
are sharply defined:
if I move I know what
all of me is from outside.

I wander and stumble around
moving and edging at things,
make coffee, peer curious
into the chrome confines
of the kettle.
I brush walls with my shoulders,
kick shins on low tables.

The pictures on the walls
are phased and changed,
their shadows trick the eye
as shadows in the hall rise
as ghosts of walls closing.

Only in the eye's corner
I catch the slow moving
of branches and leaves
caught in a white gloss

Of wood beside me,
only uneasy, sneaking around.

This is the fifth floor
above the graveyard,
blue wraps below over clean new holes.
I've watched them both dig and bury.

Fresh flowers appear,
planted rather than brought,
only sometimes, in the eye's corner,
a slow figure in a hurry.

Breeze comes with evening,
as clean as the light
and as lightly defining,
marking off, charting, skin and eyes.

Patterns evolve and whorl
in the one-coloured carpets,
twisting beneath my feet,
tangling, shifting
like water or corn.

Wide and dark-eyed I stare
at opposing windows.
The cat, black-arched,
eyes slits at my ankles.

Dark, black birds, crows, in the tree,
wings shift and croak,
always moving, clustering:
They blister the tree, shake it up,
flies around and through
wet bones in the Sun.

Only uneasy, sneaking, creeping around,
nobody's home but me,
in a way anyway.
Edging around the shades
it comes.
This kind of light could kill.

INDECISION

The wind whispers ghosts to me
Through a nearly closed window,
A sound of the world outside
Deciding what and how to be.

The night always has this,
Clouds move like doctors over the city,
Ambivalent shadows on dubious business:
Here the Moon is only a space
Showing people with wide eyes, the Earth.

Soon though, I will light a cigarette
By a window
And watch the hills
Only through tall chimneys
And smile,
Kissing smoke in long rings
Around my silence.

THE SAND GARDEN

Dead-eyed in the grit there's split green bottle glass.
The insides of our sighs share their sickly light.
Sandy-eyed
statues glare down as we pass.
Our figures grimy shadows in their scathing sight.
Too tired in this cold light to talk anymore
and no more reason to continue than before.

The city skulks deep in early smoky mist,
carnivore at the water's core, bristling, stirring,
tracing out the nature of our own tired twist.
Around tall dry towers the mists turn whispering

in dark hard lines, cutting us both cold to the core,
close into our own harsh shadows as never before.